BODIES

BODIES OF
LIGHT

Athena Kildegaard

Red Dragonfly Press
Northfield, Minnesota — 2011

ISBN 978-1-890193-36-2

Library of Congress Control Number: 2011925991

Acknowledgments are printed at the back of the book.

Printed in the United States of America on recycled stock
by BookMobile, a 100% wind-powered company

Designed and typeset by Scott King
using Menhart Pro (11pt / 15pt)

Cover painting: Michael Eble,
'Tranquil Measures,' acrylic on panel with graphite

Published by Red Dragonfly Press
307 Oxford Street
Northfield, MN 55057

www.reddragonflypress.org

Contents

This is where stories began, under the aegis of that multitude of stars which at night filch certitudes and sometimes return them as faith.

— John Berger

TENANT

Incantation: Grendel's Mother

I looked in from the elms,
looked in and wept
for there was your arm—
the fish and stars I'd inked
on your wrist, a spell
of sea and sky,
that you might live
in the fullness of earth—
the stubborn life taken out of it.
I should have screamed then,
your fingers flexed in pain.
I saw your arm
cut by those who took
what taking they could.
Men they were, passing mead
long after the moon
had made her ploy across the sky.
This flesh I watched,
their drunken visages,
hair on fire, elbows kneading
the long tables like dough
for thousand-weight loaves.
Their scythes and axes
stood against the walls,
earth treasures, wound-wares.
Your arm hung above the fire,
a hairy mallet all muscle
now drained of its salt, putrid.

They fill themselves with rancor.
They'll take and take.
Let what remains
be flame and quenching sea.

Roosters

Hi de hi de
hi de ho at dawn,
pure mojo and love
gone wrong,
a cold bed, but hearts
fierce as swords.
They're strung with lights
and last year's tinsel,
as in a basement club
where the owner—she's big
on her stool by the open door—
lifts a cumbrous chain.
They strut their stuff,
gasconnade the riffs,
grind down the thump,
the hump, the rascally
blood pound of longing
until dawn when
they step out from smoke
and spilled gin
to answer the light.

El Higado

In Batopilas, a traveller
walked into the light
and found some men
butchering a cow.
They used machetes.
The blood ran
into the mayor's yard.
The traveller asked
for the liver, el higado.
They thought it strange
how he held out
his two soft hands.
Hands that played
a tenor sax
the night before
under a canopy.
A couple danced in the rain,
their clothes so wet
they had become naked.
He held out his hands
and a man placed the liver
into the bowl of his palms.
It sought the open windows
of his curving fingers,
and he carried it before him
to his sleeping wife
in a dark back room
of the señora's boarding house.

Fox

His intestines leave his belly in a line
like a birth cord across the grass

and dew cools the fire of his fur.
From this rise I see the Domkirke.

I was meant to see it, just as, 700 years
ago, farmers and shepherds and midwives

cossetting and gentling the world around
saw it. The bells do not sound from here.

There are no flies, no smell, though
he's been here three days, grimacing.

Tomorrow after the morning fog lifts
I'll return to the small sacred chamber.

And the day after, too, until I forget
to look, or the mowers chase him away.

Walking Alone and Sore with the World

A hawk stands on air.
In the woods, a gopher,
half its head missing,
the other half maggot-plumped,
lies in the path. It smells
of ambergris or myrrh,
that rich and rare. Strange
to see this small corpse
when hawks are near.
Though the wound is old
and will not heal.

Reading the Bones

She was laid down first,
oriented toward the south,
toward warmth.

Just below her pelvis
a flint lies,
and deer's teeth trim her clavicle.
She carried the earth.

Seven others, one a grown man—
her man, we're quick to guess—
lie around her.
The man points north,
toward the waning sun,
his right arm around an infant.
Even in death, an embrace,
the comfort of it.

She lies flat, her back
to the ground,
her face covered last
on an overcast day, high summer
and dusk—that must be right—
long days the time
to return those you love,
to allow earth its sure grip
before the cold of winter
holds death still.

What Deaths We're Called To

In seventh grade I labored
  with a weak scalpel while
    my friend held the textbook diagram

like a shield between
  her face and the splayed
    carcass. I liked the viscera,

how tightly packed and tidy
  it was, one organ hugging another,
    how it all adjusted to the blade's nudges.

Not so long ago, we were looking
  at Civil War photographs, my son,
    his 7th grade friends, me turning the pages.

Here was a dead soldier,
  his mouth gaping, cherry trees
    blooming at the vanishing point.

One of the boys announced
  he'd dissected a rat that morning.
    We could smell the open wound.

At the Museum of Natural History

In this sealed jar, suspended in formaldehyde,
an infant gone awry: one leg,
no sex,

smooth as a seal, a mutiny of cells.
The child in a sac of glass
stares at us,

cheeks damp, eyelashes forever wet, one fist near its mouth.
We floated once, we could say,
but dare not.

Skin Deep

1

Imagine we could step out
like a snake, leave our skin behind.
Someone might come along
and pick it up for his collection—
skins of rattlers and garters,
the intact shell of a lobster,
conches glistening and pink inside—
what a come-on line, Come up
to see my skin? only she'd be squeamish
and afraid to admit that what she wanted most to see
was how the seam had come out—
that short blind-seam
between anus and scrotum.

2

Bound in human skin—
a hanged man, pickpocket or roustabout—
skin of book, *Fabrica Humana*,
Vesalius's magnum opus,
corpus magnanimus
taken from the grave and sliced open,
a first look at spleen and womb,
body read like ink on vellum.

3

North of the Sahara there's
trade in human skin.
Someone's left cheated
swindled of his whole hide.

4

How it gives us away,
a blush, pimples of fear—
you silly goose,
to be afraid of that—
yes baby yes yes—
How it thins with age
and tears away as easily
as peel on a boiled tomato.
How we can tell ourselves
to the world on it:
Staci 4 Ever,
tribal scars and patterns,
piercings.
How the world marks us
thief, slave, human.
How it makes room
for more of us
or less.
How it's soaked through
or gotten under.
How it hides us.

Eucalyptus

Peeling as if its life
depended on it—
in great gray ribbons—
to reveal its marbled
stateliness—a certain
shot silk mien,
a remarkable likeness
to a made thing,
though no weaver
(other than, perhaps,
a god) has put her shuttle,
no other sculptor her chisel
to its art, it stands
as if it has been standing
here longer
than memory compasses,
peeling without
diminishment, in constant
revelation, as if,
to the world, it never
gives up on the idea
that it might be revealed
as more, rather than less,
an accumulation,
rather than a reduction,
of its true self.

In Passing

"Yes, let's celebrate," she is saying
as I pass them on the library's sidewalk.
They're not holding hands. They wear
beige coats, he pulls on gloves, she takes
keys from her purse. They step
solidly, don't look at one another.
If only I could know what it is
they will celebrate. I've arrived too late.
All these details—their ruddy faces,
white hair, the coats, gloves, keys—
are revealed in a glance. Love is
like that. They lean toward one another,
the last yellow chrysanthemums in the garden.

Brothers at the Reunion

The old men stood below the exit sign
laughing and cussing as though they were
in a well-lit bar—though they'd all
given up drink years before. They cussed

for the electricity of the words. Some, widowers
who hadn't kissed a woman in years, stroked
the air with their hands. They didn't touch
one another. The one holdout blew smoke

away from their privacy. They did not talk
of faith—these men whose father had been
a deacon—they disagreed. Instead they told
the old stories about creek beds and whippings

and snakes in mailboxes. And jokes featuring
viagra and gravity. Their laughter bound them,
that and a loss of faith in their bodies,
though desire hammered there still.

The Summer You Bicycled across the Continent

That summer I stood in the closet
and smelled you in your cotton shirts
and one Goodwill sport coat. I prayed
that the relatives of the one bat I'd killed with a tennis racket
would not get in under the door. That summer
I waitressed at the Bank on the Avenue until
it went bankrupt and sent me home with no paycheck
and only enough tips, saved in a Kerr jar,
for a six-pack of Leinenkugels and twenty Marlboros.
In the bath I nearly fainted from steam and nicotine
and dreaded July and August with nothing to do but wait
for postcards from you. "I hear you look good
in a bathing suit," you talked a boy with a green crayon into
        writing
on a postcard you posted somewhere on the Blue Ridge Parkway.
And for a week, until the next card, I thought of you
imagining me in the bathing suit and that week went faster,
and the next one, too, when I walked beans with a hoe
and sang Simon and Garfunkel hits and I knew you didn't know
that I was out in a field with boys who shouted obscenities
and wore their torsos naked and sweating.

Naked

Before dawn when there are no edges,
my small son rises, takes off his pajamas.
I hear him at the side of the bed,
lift the white comforter. He comes under,
knees and belly first, vines himself
over my hip and ribs. He says
he likes to feel my skin.
I like the weight of it.

Armadillo

Vestigial, half blind, almost
unable to smell what is in her path,
the armadillo has one trick:
she fills her intestines with air
and swims to the farther shore.
Otherwise, if the stream is narrow
she lumbers along the bed,
her claws precarious on the stones,
water flowing across the carapace
that arms her pale flesh.
She tastes something like pork,
this poor swine, this humble throwback
who longs only for the naked grub,
fellow burrower, joint-tenant of the dark.

Sign for Light

Open the bedroom shutters
and let in more light. — Goethe

1

The hawk flies
on light too harsh for eyes,
on light her wings have struck.

2

A sulphurous light, molten
on oak and pane, is all
I need to play this Pathetique.
Light gilds the keys, brings alive
in gold and pain the triplets
persistent as the coming rain.

3

In the quiet after-party hour,
wine spilled and salt upon it,
trumpets like forlorn birds,
the moon is swaddled in light.

4

You come to me with the moon
on your shoulders, gossamer-
plated. My breasts are wings
alit, ablaze. They rise to meet you.

5

This alba startles,
all cock and doodle,
scratch and synchronicity,
but see how luminous
his sheeny feather,
struck by sun.

6

In the silence, monks
sign for light:
taper, lantern, wick, lamp.
Each its own sign.

In the Darwin Center, London

Around the specimen room, in glass jars
with flat tops sealed by vaseline, sea bass,
manta rays, a coelocanth, hang in formalin,
the liquid aged to amber.

Inside steel tanks ranged along the floor,
hammerheads, nurse sharks, swordfish, hide.
The sharks, the fish, as if still swimming,
are silent.

In the midst of all a giant squid floats
thick in plexiglass, lies sidewise;
the visible eye, like a medallion,
sees nothing.

The pink flesh of its eye looks precisely
like the flesh of its mantle, two tentacles,
eight legs with suction cups
on tiny stems.

The once uncanny creature verges
on decomposition; it's a mannequin,
trapped and waxy. The length of it disturbs.
And the one cool eye.

The Defiant Tableaux of October

A #10 washtub filled with turban squash
the color of granite and garnet corn,
white tissue ghosts swinging
from leaf-thinned branches, a sheaf
of corn tied beside the mailbox:
no death here, but hardly a laugh either,
something solemn and earnest, a cold-
shouldered welcome to season's end,
ghosts of summer long gone.
The red wide ribbon around stalks
of harvested corn seems a feeble
attempt at cheer. And the curve
of the washtub? The parabola of coming
and going, emptying out and filling up.

Uncle Jack Loses Half a Finger

The facts start here: Depression years,
Jack the oldest boy followed
his daddy around watching,
then later did the repairs himself
while his daddy watched. Nothing
couldn't be fixed. Moving parts
only required logic, muscle, grease
to be put right. But came a time
when things impinged. He watched clouds
as if they were hoodlums,
walked to the mailbox worrying
about a daughter's love life, fell
into bed at night with a list in his head
neon-lit and woke up already behind.
The mower quit on him mid-lawn
and the worries overrode everything
he knew about caution. Those are
the facts. The rest is a lifetime
of being reminded: when he hands
across the table a platter of chops, when he
scratches his ribs, when he waves goodbye
and then catches himself studying
what is no longer there.

Lot's Prayer

Lord, Moab and Ben-Ammi
come in from the fields
and sit beside the fire
like two hungry lions
and in their eyes is a lust
I once knew only in dreams

when I was also lion,
and a woman with skin
as white and grainy as salt
lay beneath me silent.
My spine curved above
and into her and I took her
up in my arms and legs
and bound her to me
so that nothing would come between us,
not even fear or angels
or the voice of you, Lord—
then I saw that she was salt
and I licked her
until I felt a thirst as deep as anguish.
Not a night goes by
that I do not wonder
at these boys and how they could be mine,
how out of salt they roar like lions.

No Morning More Than This

Dawn pecks at the window.
A spider toe-tips
along the lampshade's brim.
So small everything is.
Between us, the children
whisper, and the cat
cleans its paws at your feet.

Bruises

Here is the scene—
the basement of a Chicago zoo,
a locked room inside of which
screams and flails a chimpanzee;
outside the door stands the man
who brought her from the French Cameroons,
who dressed her in pinafores,
made home movies of her
riding a tricycle, feeding a baby,
then sent her off.
He has just come from the cell
where she hugged him, sobbed,
clung to his body,
moved her soft lips against his cheek.

He listens to her screeches,
stands in the cool narrow hallway
touching himself
where the chimp had touched,
as if these were bruises
and he a mother
discovering for herself the pain
of a child's needs.
As he walks down the hall,
the screams diminish—
they could be the sound
of his shoes lifting

from the clean linoleum
or the muffled whistles
of starlings in the trees.

bird tower

Fugletårn

I stood in the bird tower,
two stories up, watching,
across the inlet of the fjord,
a blue heron, my morsel,
my planet, my advocate
in the court of disappointment.
Cows bellowed below,
squelched in mud, chomped.
I couldn't stop thinking
of how someone I try to love
gave nothing. Two dozen cows
sauntered across my encircled
world, a moving queue
behind the runic bird. One cow
tried mounting another and
that was funny. The heron
was not perturbed.

One Small Thing

Yesterday on Highway 59
the Dow dropped a hundred,
tried to rally, failed.
I watched a snake
wind over the middle line.
An Israeli shot a Palestinian,
or was it the other way round?
Deer wasted in Wisconsin.
Through the rearview mirror
I watched a truck swerve—
eighteen wheels and a balanced load—
looked for the snake, too,
though not seeing it
did not stop me from rejoicing.

Public, Like a River

Children spit
from a bridge

whose girders
house brown bats.

They test the depths.
Current, current.

A white dog howls
on a sandbar.

Public, like a river,
is how I love you,

here where cottonwood seeds
rime tidepools,

and underneath, bodies
flow all rhythm.

You Are Like a Star

Even the otter finds its way
to the creek by your light.

Buds on the fig dare to open,
the thief reconsiders.

I can stand out here all night
beside the blue shed

embracing you, my hands
sure of everything they touch.

TRANSIT

Passage

This is rain
this is earth
this is where earth takes rain
this is the taking
a distillation
this is rain
become one drop
making its way
through the needle's eye
this is the cave
limestone ear hole
this is the dark
this is the one drop
worming down calcite
down the dark passage
this is the fall
water to earth to black
the black that is not seen
this is the one water
this is its arrival.

Lineage

1. In Which Something is Reported and
   Then Editorialized Upon

Erik the Red's descendants
were taken by ice. Frozen solid
the roots of their vineyards.
Burned for warmth the distaff
and the tankards. The last few,
mangled by frostbite, gnawed
at the wine casks' staves,
pretended to be drunk, or maybe
were. In their condition, who knows?
The last raven had flown
out across the turgid water,
the last wolf they'd eaten.
The last, I'm thinking, the last
of Red Erik's line blew on his
tipped fingers and waved
from the threshold of the great hall,
the enormous moving
mass of ice Freya come
to hold him again.

2. In Which the Author Recants

They'd drunk the wine weeks
before, burned the staves

and the threshold, burned every
piece that could emit even a dram
of heat, then, the one or two
remaining in the cold sat
huddled on the packed
dirt floor, tongues swollen,
lips cracked, no sign of release,
nothing but the harbinger of death,
runnelling down the vineyard.

3. In Which Something Is Reconsidered

One bit of ember
one faint glow
one descendent
spit on the coal.

4. In Which Climate is Understood to Be
   the Culprit

Those who once lived near water
now (2072) claim space in the hinterlands.
We clutch the things
we think will matter: photographs,
Shakespeare's Complete, *Life* covers,
a holy book. Because we imagine
someone will survive. Or another
species with will and memory

will come along. But no one
can agree how best to cache
our species' prizes
so they will survive
ten thousand millenia, give or take.

5. IN WHICH THE AUTHOR SUCCUMBS TO DESPAIR

The circle of the world
tightens. Runes
on the ice cannot be read
from this distance.

Cosmic Transit

Fresh from the big bang,
13.5 billion years
of traveling,
this light comes from so far
back (so many Os,
loops the tiger of time
leaps through)
(so many Os infinite
seems laughable)
and yet we're here
watching it pull in,
this transit from the cosmic
what-has-been,
on such a long trip
(how many orbits
has it passed through?
how many astral storms,
clouds of solar dust
and spiraling nebulae?)
and carrying
such a tiny suitcase
in its thin hand.
On the address tag: Beginning
(though that cannot have been
its first home)
and no known final destination.

"When that blessed light was about to leave us"

The girl falls straight down out of the too hot sky
then voilá her orange parachute goes up.

On Wednesdays the emergency siren sreees
right along the phone wires and shakes the crows up.

As for acorns, dew, and the value of love:
what comes down, it could be said, also goes up.

Walking down Bourbon Street in her spooner mood
my mother says to a whore, "Keep your toes up."

Magellan's crew stood below St. Elmo's fire,
corpus sanctum blazing, and their prayers rose up.

If you were a lonesome fly could you afford
to wait for the Venus flytrap to close up?

Boring days on the prairie, hours of black fence
standing straight until a white blizzard blows up.

The drunk steps out from rooms of funeral jazz,
holds his belly, waits until a hearse shows up.

First shave: foam, razor, our faces in the mirror—
what is it we never see as he grows up?

Bordeaux in the spring—embroidered nightgowns,
couscous in the market stalls, musk mallow's up.

Athena came into this world face down through
the birth canal, from Zeus's head she rose up.

Note: The title is a line quoted from Antonio Pigafetta's
account of Magellan's voyage around the world.

Homesick

Proserpine came up to comfort her mother.
And she could not. She lolled about the kitchen
snapping beans as if they were chicken's necks.
Nothing could make her feel again as if something
mattered. She went dancing with her friends
but under the music's bright rhythms all she heard
was a dirge. She could only shuffle past the girls
in tangerine-peel blouses and the boys
in their calculated black, to the bathroom
where she sat with hands on her knees waiting it out.
On a morning of butterflies her mother sent her
for strawberries. To the field from which
you can see the three cedars growing at an angle.
She went, an apron covering her damask skirt,
the basket on her head keeping her cool.
It was easy, so many strawberries. Bees
drunk on abundance. No one near, a silence
that seeped in under her skin. The berries
so ripe they left honey on her fingers.
She licked until her tongue hurt. Until all
was swollen and raw. She stood between
the rows, bees lolling on her ankles, and
removed apron, blouse, skirt and then lay down
naked upon the leaves, berries crushed and bleeding
into her belly, onto her thighs, against her
collarbone that formed a plow. If she could but turn
the earth and put herself down into the furrow
so that only her hair lay above,
a plant bursting with fruit, home, home, home.

Traveling Light

My father and his seven brothers sat—
the eve of their mother's funeral—
so they could look each other in the eye
and not mistake their words for sighs.

I found, that morning, in her guest-room desk
a billfold kept for thirty years,
the black and cracking leather hip-curved still.
The brothers passed it palm to palm

unfolding it and taking out—each one
with hands as big as his, and faith—
the gas receipt and voter's card. My dad
said how the gas was for a trip

to visit us, just months before his father's death.
They drove across the snow-packed plains
below the Vs of geese and stopped somewhere
to fill the tank and check the map.

He wore a slender tie and she a pin
that held a scarf in place. A gift
my father sent ten years before from France,
on leave and sick for home.

The sun made of their car a silhouette
that rode along the stippled fields
where geese had stopped to feed on corn
before their long trip home.

In This Late Light

Against the new shorn field
the pheasant cock's breast glows.
His mate is close, though hidden
by wild honeysuckle. Beloved,
only this morning I hurt you.
Through binoculars, I see
how his white collar flashes
against the red. And now
the earth has turned,
she doesn't appear, his color fades.
All we could want changes.

Last Night in Mississippi

Along this vining creek
crickets vie for wavelengths, my friend
has gone inside to her almost teenager
budding in the night, and I stand
a totem of silence, of having-gone.
Back for a visit I've been afraid to say
anything, it might come out all twisted
like a kerchief knotted twice too much.
It's been raining all day. Grass cowers,
magnolia blooms brim to collapse.
She's gone inside to her dishwasher
and the dog that needs a bath, to her
husband quiet as porcelain. I stand
where I can hear the loblollies creak
and complain, the wind shake down
the white oaks. It's all a crime.
That we cannot stay in one place.
That we cannot leave when we should,
because we're afraid or we're slow
with ourselves. I stand here
in the muggy night trying to hold
onto it, in case I don't return.
The blue hydrangea droops. Already
I'm forgetting the things I meant to say.

King Pierus to His Daughters

King Pierus challenged the Muses to a singing contest
with his nine daughters. When the daughters lost, Apollo
changed them to magpies.

I see you in the cypress,
your tail feathers fluffed
by a half-earth wind, and
all that you have hoarded:
your mother's brooch,
the stylus from the metronome,
knicks and knacks you've
chattered over for months,
pieces of my greed-heavy heart.
What can I say, my pica-picas,
my noisy songstresses,
to make up for my pride?
Your raspy queg queg queg
punishes enough, that and your songs
I am loathe to remember.

Deaf Smith County, 1932

Trains ground through day and night
loaded with grain and hoof and hoboes.
No one got off, no one boarded;
Herefords and winter wheat held
everyone in place. And the dust storms.

She lay wet dishcloths over the crib
and dust fell in silica layers, forming
a thin board for schoolboys' sums,
fingernails in the dust scratching through
to damp-darkened cloth, my father's
brothers glossing this asthma tent
with hognoses and hangmen's nooses
and the name of the oldest brother's beloved.

So that he, my father, breathed
in that small place, watched the shapes
and scrawls come and go, all backwards,
crabbed and faint. Once, I watched him
put everything he'd ever written in a fire,
words to flame to dust, so he could start again.

Geese on the Horizon

The landscape's on fire,
even the field of bristly hay
seems brave. I've filled
my bag with words
thinking to lighten my load.
A cat with white ears watches
me, solemn as uncut pages.
Five hundred geese rise
at my footstep. Can I be
a secret? or must I burn
like the maples and oaks?
The geese, hungry and loud,
pull me toward the horizon.

After Harvest

Across the pond magpies line a tractor's wake,
then rise and sheer off over the water, over
two boys who carry fishing poles parallel to the earth.
Their shadows cast a hieroglyph meaning "idleness"
or "possibility." The one depending on the other.
They lay their poles in the dirt and look for thin rocks.
The tractor is blue and pulls red discs. Sunlight
sharpens against the tractor's window. The tractor pulls
and pulls through the black dirt. The boys send rocks
across the pond's clouded surface, the rocks push the water
out into rings. Now the magpies circle back. The boys press
hooks through worms, then send them out in a wide arc.

Anniversary

You told me how church bells
woke you well before dawn
and you counted yourself alert:
forty resonating knocks at day's door.
Then you lay under the narrow sheet
beside your wife, beside an open window,
the night sky opened out, thinking of how,
the day before, she'd held a bouquet
of dried flowers—arañas, margaritas—
and then of how her eyes turned up
to find you. How change comes
and doesn't—she'd found you the same
over a bouquet of fresh roses a year go—
like the light of a star that's there
and not there. Who are we now?
The star: see how it finds you.

Swans

Two white bodies float—
heads and necks tucked away—
as though anchored, like buoys
marking a safe passage.
In this cold damp no boats
cut along the fjord; no wind
blows, even gulls roost.
I'm out alone, restless,
not even sure of my foothold
on this rocky beach. There's
someone else, a thin presence
on the narrow point,
someone leaning, as I am,
toward the current.

Translation

On a rock over the water hyacinth
facing away from the setting sun
a great blue heron stood runic.
To move would have been a translation
of wings from the language of water
and stone, of coursing across
permanence, to the language
of sky, wind, clouds, the realm
of uncertainty.
            Impatient, my mind
on the tasks of dailiness, I turned away,
but hesitated (that's all!) and turned
back to stone, to white flowers,
to the heron already flown.

Swallow's Proof

A swallow kept her nest outside my window
in the cornice of wooden rafters. I saw her
tucked into that neat architecture of mud,
her pale eggs warm as my cheek on the pillow.
I'd gone off alone to write. Only there I was
with that bird, her homely thrift, quick beak,
everything about her efficient. Even in my dream
she swooped and stalled. I couldn't let go of her,
the curve of her wings a tidy calligraphy,
a fine jointure, proof of my own stalled heart.

After Reading a Line by Brother Jacob, a 17th Century Dane Who Lived Among the Purépecha

"...and never touched wine, not even in snowy weather."

Though when frost rimes the glazing
and the trek for wood requires coat,
sweater, scarf and high boots, then a glass

of burgundy pungent and almost viscous
would seem a cure for melancholy,
the sense of loss brought on even

before the snow, on that day in early
autumn when a wind from the northeast
snuck in below your sleeve to measure

your heartbeat and found it annoyingly
regular. It was on that day you bought
the bottle, slipped it onto the rack,

saying to yourself how it would comfort
on a bleak February evening, a fire bringing
up the temperature, your feet in wool

and the whole evening lying
before you without purpose. It was then
you packed your heart for winter.

Middle Age

Late afternoon, the crickets' vibrato songs
like urgent telegrams from the frontier
announce the summer's longest day.
Already we're waiting for rain
and the tomatoes haven't set their fruit,
the lilies arch, heavy with tight blossoms.
We sit on the patio with our gin and tonics,
the grass expectant before us. Children
should be here, in bright suits,
leaping through arcs of water. Instead
they're older, loosed and off with friends,
and we sit in the shade, listening.

Raccoon

Early night along Highway 7
our headlights fell on two raccoons
crossing to the creek's wider banks.
The mother hurried before the light,
her cub lingered.

From inside the car it sounded like a bag of towels,
or a rubber ball tossed below the wheels.
That moment—on a two-lane highway
between loblollies and pin oaks,
with night filling all the bowls of silence—
could not simply come and go.

My daughter wept in the back seat.
I reached behind, touched her knee to ease her,
to ease myself through what I tried to say about misfortune.
Later, in the night, she sneaked beside me in the bed
and pressed her feet against my thighs,
chewed the sleep clean in her mouth.

Out of a Dream

tu boca, salida de tu sueño
me dio el sabor de tierra, de agua marina — Pablo Neruda

When your hands woke my skin,
my breasts, pulled my hip toward you
and you spoke to me in Spanish, I realized

that you were still in Ometepe,
still crossing the lake under tin sky,
the boat keeling, an old woman wearing your coat;

the children cried into their mother's palms and the waves
climbed into the boat, soaking even the backs of knees,
and you turned to find the horizon,

to find land warm, like flesh, only more
than flesh, so you came out of the water
and I made you talk again, "el agua . . .

el barco . . . los niños gritaron al cielo . . .",
as if words could wake me enough to bear
you through to the sleep that came after.

Under the Pepper Trees

My mother sat in an iron chair on the patio
of a rented house and garden in a quiet village
reached only with the help of a child
who knew his way over a pot-holed road
between the stands of sugar cane and pepper trees.
Her book lay folded open, spine up on the table.
She could hardly breathe. Even walking to the bathroom
turned her gray: it took less energy to wait.
I watched her take her glasses off, then put them on,
off, on, rub her eyes in the sun, watch us
and take them off again.
We played in a shallow spring-fed pool, my children,
my father, too far for her to hear us
as we teased and giggled, as my father and I broke
through the children's patter with talk
of Tolstoy and Dostoevsky, those two divines
who shared the same mad half century.
Her lungs had dried up like two curled maple leaves,
all the red washed out until everything—watching her
    grandchildren,
listening for something to laugh at, even sitting
with her back against the cool iron—demanded of her body
more than she could muster. Beyond the wall, under pepper trees,
men sang and talked. Boys sat in the branches. The women stood
in knee-deep water washing cotton shirts and school dresses.
Everyone helped carry the damp clothes down the path,
under the trees, under the dusky sky, through the breeze

that turned the sugar cane to guitars and tenor voices,
    everyone alight
with the pleasures of cleanliness, of a day at the cool water,
everyone not remembering despair, not remembering
that any breath we take could be our last.

Ripe Cherries

I read that the men,
on their way to Gettysburg,
stopped along the road
to pick and eat ripe cherries.

That the fruit should not
go to waste.

That they should take
such pleasure before battle.

That the oldest among them
should shake the trees
and the youngest gather
the fallen fruit.
That they should aim rifles
with the taste of cherries
against their teeth.

After the Death of His Brother's Wife

Uncle Jack, the oldest, says,
From now on it's a lottery.
He means, Don't count on me
to die next. I may be the oldest,
I may have lied before any of you,
gotten drunk first, fucked a girl first,
but this time, boys, don't count on me.

Maybe they would whisper,
Jack, show us the way,
as if the way were visible,
something other
than the brightest darkness,
an unfolding of a flat thing,
a certainty weighed against itself.

What he means is, I'm afraid—
and if they could, his brothers
would say to him Yes, yes—

Idyll

A tall man, split-rail hard,
and another, middling,
passed my house carrying azaleas,
the blooms bright pink, tendrils
of root dangling from the pots.

That was years ago and yet
I see them still, their striding
toward the cemetery, the tall one
holding his pot away from his white shirt,
the other hugging the blooms to his heart,

neither speaking. Did they hear
the mockingbird carolling in the privet?
I'm waiting for them to return,
empty-handed, sweaty in the humid
afternoon, but bearing news.

Mother's Prayer

I stood on the porch of our raised cottage
      and saw my two ruddy children
crouched below in the grass
      over a hard-backed beetle
and I was taken with this phobia
      that goes up and up with me
and suddenly I saw myself fallen,
      my body twisted on the pavement,
a thigh bare and scraped and bloody,
      and my two children, wooden
with fear, bent over me
      saying softly, "Mama, mama."

And I knew then, as one comes to know
      things that lodge themselves in us,
that I had no way of telling them,
      my children, how I would
leave them some day as ashes
      they will toss out over moving water,
how they will feel abandoned
      in ways that even dreams cannot express.
Lord, make room inside me for this.

In the Kirkegård, December

The graves here are swaddled with pine boughs
and across the street a woman lights tall candles.
In her window a white orchid blooms.

Men working on a steep roof
came down some time ago—I saw them
at noon, when the sun crested the chimney

—they left the ladders for tomorrow. How easy
it seems—now when daylight is lean
and weather tears at the sky—to stand

balanced before death, to warm a room
with only three flames and a flower.
Someone has been paid to lay the boughs

in quilted patterns around the stones,
—the sticky resin and sharp smell of Yule—
to tuck in the dead, the beloved strangers, for winter.

Moon

Fifty years ago we saw the dark side
of the moon, not as mind-blowing as Herschel
finding Uranus since the commutative property
suggested that that side would be much like this,
and the poets continued unperturbed,
continued celebrating her whiteness,
her coy coming and going, the way
she reassured us of what we couldn't see.

And now the moon's grown closer still,
we've trod upon her, measured her, gathered her
to take away with us, in our pockets, as it
were, but still she bares her lightness, how
well she looks, while we grow old and gravity
commutes us nearer, nearer to the dark.

Aria

Mimi died once in our family room.
My mother opened her throat
not to sing but to keep the keen
back, protect her children
from her deepest regret.

Mimi died in the opera house
rigged out to sail across Sydney Harbor.
She died at the Palacio de Bellas Artes
where a dapper-suited man
sang along, his tears turned to melody.

Mimi died again in New Orleans.
Something burst against my ribs
afterwards, crossing the parking lot.
I swore it off. No more Bohemians
in their turreted poverty.

No more violins, their strings
the sinews of Rodolfo's heart.
No more gelida manina, it would kill me, too.
But that was a lie.
The way we lie sometimes

to cover up for what we know
will again break inside us—
not a breaking that leaves shards
or wounds, but breaking as the sun does
into darkness, as joy breaks from our tears.

Departure

Leave nothing behind: leave
no trace: of how you stood
just here catching your breath:
of the yellow mums you planted
beneath the porch's overhanging
eaves: of whiffle balls lost in the privet:
of the time you lay in the grass
looking for Hesperides: or when
Philip read Hayden in the dark:
or the crumbs you shook from
the tablecloth and left for birds:
leave no footprint: thumbprint:
no breath mist on the windowpane:
leave nothing because going
is going: because goodbye is
like a long trailer driving off
with everything in it: even memories:
flapping behind like scarves:
threatening to catch beneath
the wheels: and pull you down:

One Forged Note

The concrete-lined copper box they pulley
a coffin into weighs 5000 pounds.

If you could have your coffin lowered
into something other than concrete,
what would you choose?
goose down, purple velvet, hand-painted ceramic?
Would you choose oak planks hewed from the tree that kept
the north wind out of your childhood bedroom?
Or would you leave it unlined
so that your casket would bump down onto the copper case
and the whole thing reverberate in a resonant major key
just the way you always wanted to sing,
your diaphragm filling with air and then pushing the sound
up and out in one deep tone, one forged note,
and you feel your sinuses expand
and the space vibrate and the pressure
behind your eyeballs make you blind to all
that you have ever witnessed, all that you have ever
wanted to see but didn't dare,
all that you never saw and couldn't know
you'd never seen, all that you saw even before
sight or knowing or the heavy obligation
of being witness came full upon you.

To Make an Accounting of Mysteries

Begin with the minute you fell from the sky,
from the stamen of your father's yearning,
pistils bursting from the unfurling petals.
From there arrival and departure, ritual and whim,
and spare moments when your heart
reels, its release joy, an embrace of leaf fall,
wind rush, the engine of the universe
cranking and starting and you witness the how,
the why that leaves you shocked, but later
you can't summon it and have only to await
the next. Sure it comes, this ratcheted revolution,
because the piston of your heart can bear
only so much pressure, so much of the quotidian
before it bursts again. Measure by epiphany.

Acknowledgments

I gratefully acknowledge the editors of the following journals where these poems first appeared:

Bateau: "After Reading a Line by Brother Jacob, a 17th Century Dane Who Lived Among the Purépecha"

Blaze: "Armadillo," "Deaf Smith Country, 1932," "Roosters"

The Blueroad Reader: "The Summer You Bicycled Across the Continent," "Cosmic Transit"

Cream City Review: "Brothers at the Reunion"

Defined Providence: "Raccoon"

Faultline: "Passage"

Flyway: "Naked"

ForPoetry.com: "Eucalyptus," "Homesick," "Lot's Prayer"

ISLE: "Translation," "Geese on the Horizon"

Knockout: "Swans"

The Malahat Review: "Under the Pepper Trees," "When that blessed light was about to leave us"

Otter Tail Review: "One Forged Note," "Sign for Light," "Last Night in Mississippi"

Poetry East: "Ripe Cherries," "One Small Thing," "In Passing"

Seattle Review: "Incantation"

Tar River Poetry: "After Harvest"

The Texas Observer: "After the Death of His Brother's Wife"

Valparaiso Poetry Review: "Middle Age," "In the Kirkegård"

Willow Springs: "El Higado," "Aria," "Mother's Prayer"

Yalobusha Review: "Out of a Dream," "Bruises"

"After the Death of His Brother's Wife" also appeared in *To Sing Along the Way: Minnesota Women Poets from Pre-Territorial Days to the Present.*

"Aria" also appeared in *Letters to the World: Poems from the Wom-po Listserv*

And with deep gratitude I thank Lise Kildegaard, the muses of WompWorks, and most of all and always, Arne.

About the Author

Athena Kildegaard was born in Wyoming, grew up in Minnesota, and has lived in Sydney Australia, Chicago, Austin Texas, Oxford Mississippi, New Orleans, and Guanajuato Mexico. She now lives in Morris out west there a ways in Minnesota where she is a lecturer at the University of Minnesota, Morris. Her first book of poems, *Rare Momentum*, is also a Red Dragonfly Press book. She is the recipient of grants from the Lake Region Arts Council and the Minnesota State Arts Board.